The 2012 - 2013 Notre Dame Fighting Irish:

Undefeated Season, BCS Championship, & a College Football Legacy

Dan Fathow

Megalodon Entertainment, LLC.

Published by Megalodon Entertainment, LLC. (USA)
www.MegalodonEntertainment.com

First Printing: January 2013

Printed in the United States of America.

ISBN: 978-1-61589-039-2
ISBN-10: 1-61589-039-4

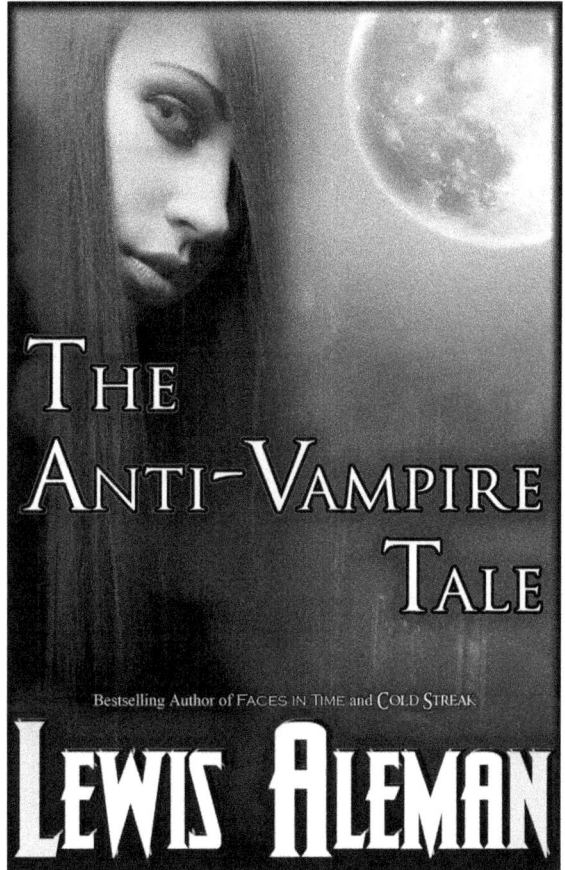

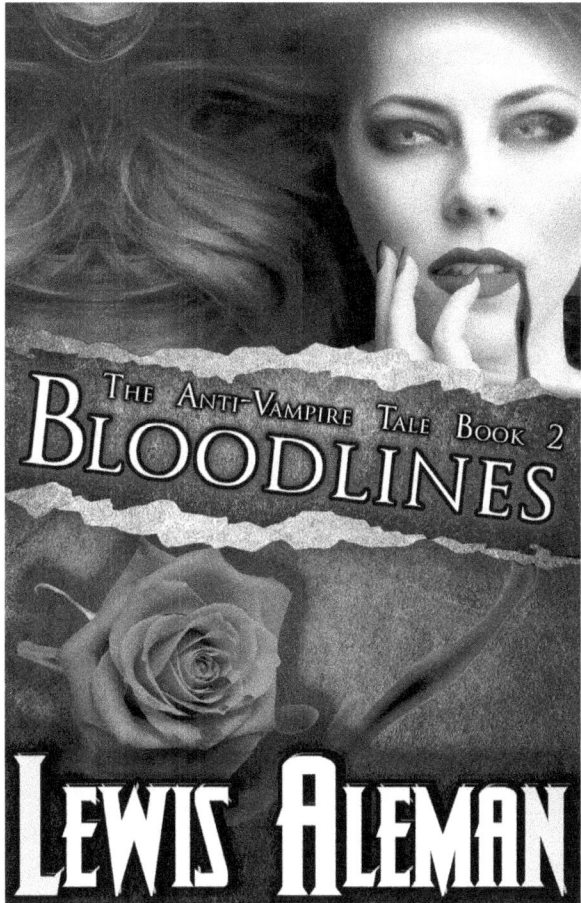

The
2012 - 2013
Notre Dame
Fighting
Irish:

Undefeated Season, BCS Championship, & a College Football Legacy

Dan Fathow

Megalodon Entertainment, LLC.

TABLE OF CONTENTS

PART I: 2012 THE MAGNIFICENT SEASON

PART II: THE BCS NATIONAL CHAMPIONSHIP THE MATCHUP VS. ALABAMA

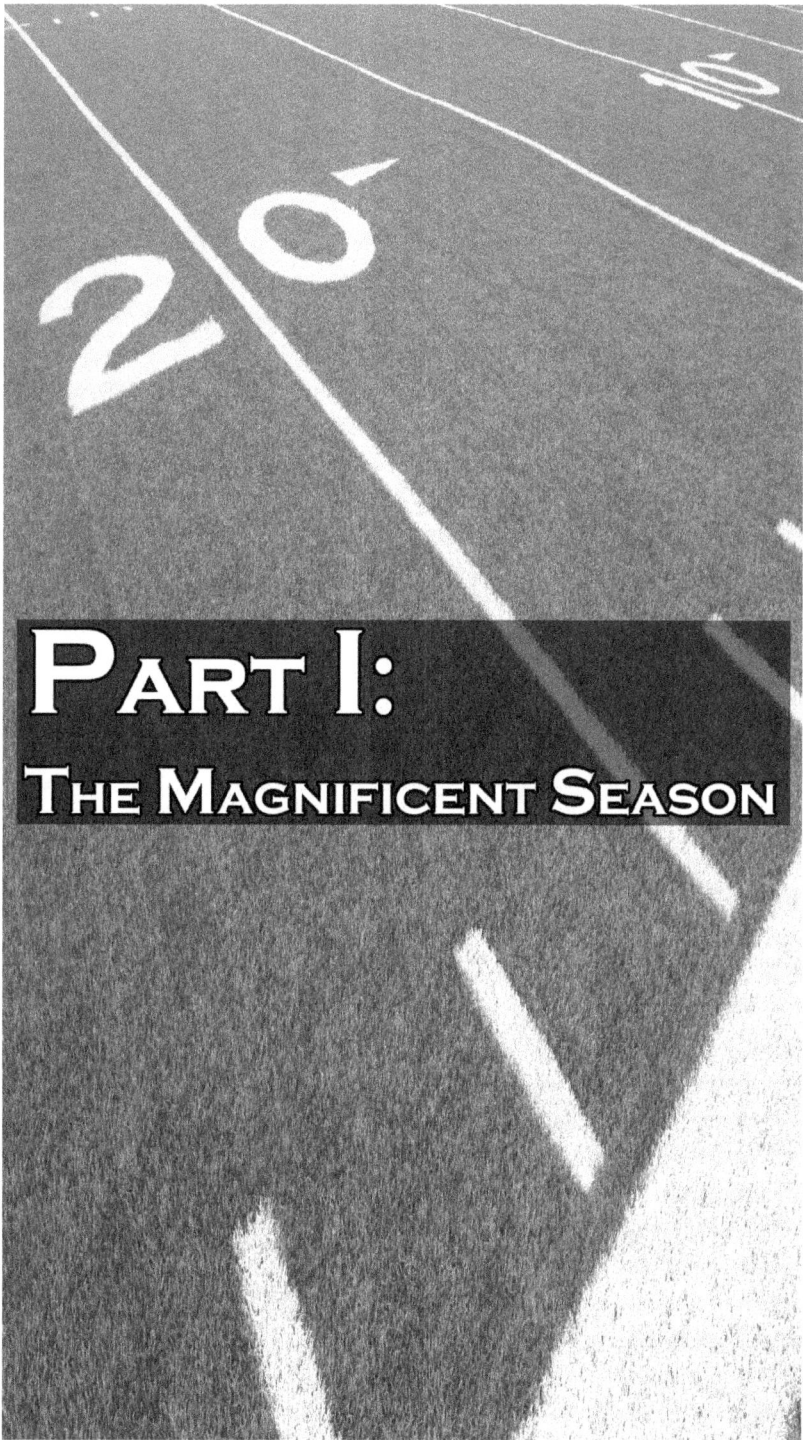

PART I:
THE MAGNIFICENT SEASON

GAME 1

September 1, 2012
Aviva Stadium – Dublin, Ireland

Teams	1st	2nd	3rd	4th	Total
Navy	0	3	7	0	10
Notre Dame	13	14	13	10	50

GAME SUMMARY

This game was notable for a lot of reasons. First, Notre Dame, who would end the season as the #1-ranked team in the country, started the season off as an unranked team. Second, this game took place in Dublin, Ireland in front of a crowd of 49,000 people*.

(*ESPN - http://espn.go.com/ncf/recap?id=322452426)

In addition to those outside circumstances, the Fighting Irish were debuting their new quarterback, Everett Golson, and due to a violation of team rules, Notre Dame's star running back, Cierre Wood, was suspended and missing from the game. Those two elements alone are enough variables to create disaster; however, this did not happen at all.

Golson had a good first game, throwing for 144 yards, 1 touchdown and 1 interception. While not a record-setting performance by any means, it was an encouraging start for a new quarterback. Couple that with a 40-point victory, and it was a fantastic start for Notre Dame.

The Fighting Irish's running game showed up in force, accounting for 293 yards and 5 touchdowns, 4 of them split evenly between Theo Riddick and George Atkinson III. The receiving end also did their job with 197 yards and 1 touchdown. All in all, it was a pretty balanced outing for a team with a new QB and missing a star running back.

Everett Golson's job as the starting quarterback was not guaranteed at this point in the season. Tommy Rees, the previous starter from the year before, was due to return the next week, so Golson needed to make a statement to hang on to his starting spot on the team.

TEAM LEADERS

Passing

Everett Golson #5
144 Yards, 1 Touchdown, 1 Interception
(12/18, 66.67 Comp %)

Andrew Hendrix #12
53 Yards, 0 Touchdowns, 0 Interceptions
(4/5, 80 Comp %)

Rushing

Theo Riddick #6
107 Yards on 19 Carries
10.09 Yards per Carry
2 Touchdowns

George Atkinson III #4
99 Yards on 9 Carries
11 Yards per Carry
2 Touchdowns

Cam McDaniel #33
59 Yards on 9 Carries
6.56 Yards per Carry
0 Touchdowns

Andrew Hendrix #12
20 Yards on 6 Carries
3.33 Yards per Carry
1 Touchdown

Receiving

DaVaris Daniels #10
49 Yards on 2 Receptions
24.5 Yards per Reception
0 Touchdowns

Troy Niklas #85
29 Yards on 1 Reception
29 Yards per Reception
0 Touchdown Receptions

Theo Riddick #6
25 Yards on 2 Reception
12.5 Yards per Reception
0 Touchdown Reception

Tyler Eifert #80
22 Yards on 4 Reception
5.5 Yards per Reception
1 Touchdown Reception

Kicking

Nick Tausch #40
8 Points Total
1/1 Field Goals
5/6 Extra Points

Interceptions

Manti Te'o #5
1 Interception

THE BOTTOM LINE

1 - 0

GAME 2

September 8, 2012
Notre Dame Stadium – Notre Dame, IN

Teams	1st	2nd	3rd	4th	Total
Purdue	0	7	0	10	17
#22 Notre Dame	0	7	10	3	20

GAME SUMMARY

After the previous week's trouncing of Navy, Notre Dame started to gain some recognition, getting into the rankings at #22.

The most talked about aspect of the game was Everett Golson throwing for an impressive 289 yards with 1 touchdown and 1 interception. On top of that passing effort, Golson ran in a touchdown himself. Despite that impressive 2nd-start performance, Golson was taken out of the game in favor of experience for the last drive.

The game-winning drive came from former starter Tommy Rees who was then back from his 1-game suspension. Rees was suspended for being arrested at an off-campus party earlier in the year, back in May. Rees came off the bench with the Fighting Irish tied with the unranked Purdue Boilermakers at 17-17. Rees converted on 2 important 3rd down situations to get within field goal range for kicker Kyle Brindza to put the ball between the uprights to win the game.

More game highlights were the 2 interceptions made by Notre Dame corner back Bennett Jackson.

Notre Dame beat Purdue in total yards 376 to 288. While the Fighting Irish dominated the passing game, 324 yards to the Boilermakers' 198, Purdue had nearly double the rushing yards of Notre Dame, 90 yards to 52 yards. The Fighting Irish won the turnover battle 2-1. Penalties were nearly even between both teams, each with 8 penalties, and Notre Dame only giving up 1 more penalty yard than their opponent.

While Purdue was 3-3 on 4th down conversions (Notre Dame did not go for it on 4th down during this game), the Fighting Irish were the clear winners on 3rd-down efficiency with an impressive 11 of 19, where the Boilermakers were only good on 6 of 17.

TEAM LEADERS

Passing

Everett Golson #5
289 Yards, 1 Touchdown, 0 Interceptions
(21/31, 67.74 Comp %)

Tommy Rees #11
35 Yards, 0 Touchdowns, 0 Interceptions
(3/6, 50 Comp %)

Rushing

Theo Riddick #6
53 Yards on 15 Carries
3.53 Yards per Carry
0 Touchdowns

Everett Golson #5
-10 Yards on 16 Carries
-0.625 Yards per Carry
1 Touchdown

Receiving

Tyler Eifert #80
98 Yards on 4 Receptions
24.5 Yards per Reception
0 Touchdown Reception

DaVaris Daniels #10
70 Yards on 4 Receptions
17.5 Yards per Reception
0 Touchdown Receptions

Theo Riddick #6
44 Yards on 4 Receptions
11 Yards per Reception
0 Touchdown Receptions

T.J. Jones #7
20 Yards on 3 Receptions
6.67 Yards per Reception
1 Touchdown Reception

Kicking

Kyle Brindza #27
8 Points Total
2/3 Field Goals
2/2 Extra Points

Interceptions

Bennett Jackson #2
2 Interceptions

THE BOTTOM LINE

2 - 0

GAME 3

September 15, 2012
Spartan Stadium – East Lansing, MI

Teams	1st	2nd	3rd	4th	Total
#10 Michigan State	0	3	0	0	**3**
#20 Notre Dame	7	7	0	6	**20**

GAME SUMMARY

Week 3 proved to be the first true test for the fighting Irish as they met #10-ranked Michigan State on the road in Spartan Stadium. Notre Dame came into this game ranked #20.

Notre Dame was not generally expected to win this game, so a 20-3 beating of the Spartans caught national attention for the Fighting Irish. They were rapidly proving themselves to a system that had not even ranked them when the season began, and by the 3rd game, they were climbing their way through the top 20.

After Tommy Rees was brought in to secure the win the previous week against Purdue, there was some speculation over who would be the starting quarterback in this contest. Everett Golson was named the starting quarterback and finished the game, leading his team to a decisive victory.

Everett Golson threw for 178 yards and 1 touchdown with no interceptions. His completion percentage was only

43.75, but his team was never in danger of losing this game. Once again, Golson ran in a touchdown himself on top of his passing efforts.

The Notre Dame running game had a somewhat disappointing day, putting up 122 total yards, and the only rushing touchdown came from the quarterback.

The Fighting Irish won the turnover battle 1-0, as well as taking more total yards: 300 to 237. One of the hidden factors in this game was 4th-down efficiency. While the Spartans went 0-2 on 4th down, Notre Dame went 1-2. Failed 4th down conversions are often more crushing for morale than for statistics. Converting on 4th down is a shot in the arm for any offense because it takes confidence on the part of the coaching staff and skill on the part of the players to pull it off under pressure. Conversely, failing to do so is demoralizing for both players and the coaching staff.

TEAM LEADERS

Passing

Everett Golson #5
178 Yards, 1 Touchdown, 0 Interceptions
(14/32, 43.75 Comp %)

Rushing

Cierre Wood #20
56 Yards on 10 Carries
5.6 Yards per Carry
0 Touchdowns

George Atkinson III #4
43 Yards on 5 Carries
8.6 Yards per Carry
0 Touchdowns

Theo Riddick #6
30 Yards on 12 Carries
2.5 Yards per Carry
0 Touchdowns

Everett Golson #5
7 Yards on 3 Carries
2.33 Yards per Carry
1 Touchdown

Receiving

T.J. Jones #7
59 Yards on 4 Receptions
2.53 Yards per Reception
0 Touchdowns

Robby Toma #9
58 Yards on 5 Receptions
11.6 Yards per Reception
0 Touchdown Receptions

John Goodman #81
36 Yards on 1 Reception
36 Yards per Reception
1 Touchdown Reception

Theo Riddick #6
25 Yards on 2 Receptions
12.5 Yards per Reception
0 Touchdown Receptions

Kicking

Kyle Brindza #27
8 Points Total
2/2 Field Goals
2/2 Extra Points

Interceptions

None

THE BOTTOM LINE

3 - 0

GAME 4

September 22, 2012
Notre Dame Stadium – Notre Dame, IN

Teams	1st	2nd	3rd	4th	Total
#18 Michigan	0	0	0	6	**6**
#11 Notre Dame	0	10	0	3	**13**

GAME SUMMARY

Game 4 marked the 2nd week in a row that Notre Dame faced a ranked opponent, this time in the form of the #18-ranked Michigan Wolverines. Going into this game, Notre Dame moved up in the rankings to #11, based on their destruction of the Spartans in the previous week.

While this game was predominantly a defensive battle with neither team scoring in the 1st or 3rd quarters, this game proved to be a shining moment for the Fighting Irish's defense, as they nearly shut out the Wolverines, who did not score at all until the 4th quarter.

Quarterback duties were split in this game between Tommy Rees and Everett Golson. Rees put up much better numbers as he went 8 for11 for 115 yards with 0 interceptions, while Golson went 3 for 8 for 30 yards and 2 interceptions. Neither quarterback threw for a touchdown reception, although Rees did run in a touchdown himself.

What really won this game for the Fighting Irish were the 5 staggering interceptions by its defense and its solid kicking game, which accounted for 7 of its 13 points.

TEAM LEADERS

Passing

Tommy Rees #11
115 Yards, 0 Touchdowns, 0 Interceptions
(8/11, 72.73 Comp %)

Everett Golson #5
30 Yards, 0 Touchdowns, 2 Interceptions
(3/8, 3.75 Comp %)

Rushing

Theo Riddick #6
52 Yards on 17 Carries
3.05 Yards per Carry
0 Touchdowns

Cierre Wood #20
39 Yards on 7 Carries
5.57 Yards per Carry
0 Touchdowns

George Atkinson III #4
4 Yards on 4 Carries
1 Yard per Carry
0 Touchdowns

Tommy Rees #11
2 Yards on 1 Carries
2 Yards per Carry
1 Touchdown

Receiving

T.J. Jones #7
59 Yards on 4 Receptions
2.53 Yards per Reception
0 Touchdowns

Robby Toma #9
58 Yards on 5 Reception
11.6 Yards per Reception
0 Touchdown Receptions

John Goodman #81
36 Yards on 1 Reception
36 Yards per Reception
1 Touchdown Reception

Theo Riddick #6
25 Yards on 2 Receptions
12.5 Yards per Reception
0 Touchdown Receptions

Kicking

Kyle Brindza #27
7 Points Total
2/2 Field Goals
1/1 Extra Points

Interceptions

Manti Te'o #5
2 Interceptions

KeiVarae Russell #6
1 Interception

Bennett Jackson #2
1 Interception

Nicky Baratti #29
1 Interception

THE BOTTOM LINE

4 - 0

GAME 5

September 29, 2012
Soldier Field – Chicago, IL

Teams	1st	2nd	3rd	4th	Total
Miami (Florida)	3	0	0	0	**3**
#9 Notre Dame	7	6	21	7	**41**

GAME SUMMARY

The Fighting Irish came into game 5 ranked up to #9 in the nation as they met an unranked Miami (Florida) team, who came into the game at 4-1.

Notre Dame was certainly the favorite in this contest, but not many were expecting the 41-3 slaughter that ensued.

The Fighting Irish defense had another impressive day, allowing the Miami Hurricanes a field goal in the first quarter and then goose-egging them for the rest of the game.

Everett Golson had a much improved game going 17 of 22 for 186 yards with no interceptions. Tommy Rees also saw a little action as he went 2 for 4 for 25 yards and 0 interceptions. Neither quarterback threw a touchdown pass in this game.

So where did the 41 whopping points come from? 5 rushing touchdowns accounted for 30 of the points, and the kicking game provided 11 more points via 2 field goals on 3 attempts and 5 of 5 extra points.

In total, Notre Dame's offense accounted for an impressive 587 yards, while holding the Hurricanes to just 201 total yards. When you rack up nearly 3 times the yards as your opponent while not giving up a single turnover, you're going to win, and usually you're going to win *big*, as in this 38-point deficit.

Team Leaders

Passing

Everett Golson #5
186 Yards, 0 Touchdowns, 0 Interceptions
(17/22, 77.27 Comp %)

Tommy Rees #11
25 Yards, 0 Touchdowns, 0 Interceptions
(2/4, 50 Comp %)

Rushing

George Atkinson III #4
123 Yards on 10 Carries
12.3 Yard per Carry
1 Touchdown

Cierre Wood #20
118 Yards on 18 Carries
6.56 Yards per Carry
2 Touchdowns

Cam McDaniel #33
21 Yards on 5 Carries
4.20 Yards per Carry
1 Touchdown

Theo Riddick #6
21 Yards on 5 Carries
4.20 Yards per Carry
1 Touchdown

Receiving

DeVaris Daniels #10
48 Yards on 3 Receptions
16 Yards per Reception
0 Touchdown Receptions

T.J. Jones #7
45 Yards on 4 Receptions
11.25 Yards per Reception
0 Touchdown Receptions

Tyler Eifert #80
31 Yards on 2 Receptions
15.50 Yards per Reception
0 Touchdowns

Robby Toma #9
22 Yards on 2 Receptions
11 Yards per Reception
0 Touchdown Receptions

Kicking

Kyle Brindza #27
11 Points Total
2/3 Field Goals
5/5 Extra Points

Interceptions

None

THE BOTTOM LINE

5 - 0

GAME 6

October 13, 2012
Notre Dame Stadium – Notre Dame, IN

Teams	1st	2nd	3rd	4th	OT	Total
#17 Stanford	0	10	0	3	0	13
#7 Notre Dame	3	0	0	10	7	20

GAME SUMMARY

Week 6 proved to be a monumental test for the 5-0 Fighting Irish as they faced a determined 4-1 Stanford team that had had Notre Dame's number for the past 3 years.

This game proved to be an exciting, overtime nail-biter that ended with Notre Dame moving up to 6-0 and Stanford Cardinal falling to 4-2, which would turn out to be the last time Stanford lost all season, ending up 12-2 (beating 2 different #2-ranked teams in the process). So, Stanford was a much better team than their 17th-ranking implied, as they finished the season ranked #6. This was a huge win for Notre Dame and all of its fans, but in retrospect, it was an even more important and bigger win than most realized at the time.

An interesting aspect of this game was that Tommy Rees once again came off the bench to lead the Fighting Irish to victory. Rees came in on the first overtime possession, leading a drive that culminated in a 7-yard touchdown pass to T.J. Jones to give Notre Dame the 20-13 lead. Stanford drove the ball down the field into a first-and-goal situation on Notre Dame's 4-yard line. The first 3 plays by Stanford on this goal-line stand accounted for a little more than 3 yards, leaving them inside the 1-yard line on 4th down. Stanford ran again, and Notre Dame held and pushed back. The play was a bit controversial as some thought Stanford's running back Stepfan Taylor did indeed score the touchdown even though he was called down. The play was reviewed, and the call was upheld. So, the Notre Dame Fighting Irish were the victors, continuing along on their way to an unbeaten season.

While this game is remembered mostly for its Hollywood-style finish, there were other factors that contributed to its outcome. Notre Dame took the worse-end of the turnover battle giving up 3 lost fumbles to Stanford's 2 interceptions.

The Fighting Irish had 3 more penalties than their opposition, but it only added up to 5 more penalty yards. So, the penalty damage was about even between the teams.

Notre Dame won total yards with 334 yards to Stanford's 272. Both teams were 0 and 1 on 4th-down conversions, and they were nearly identical on 3rd-down efficiency with Notre Dame edging out Stanford with 7 of 16 to 6 of 16.

TEAM LEADERS

Passing

Everett Golson #5
141 Yards, 1 Touchdown, 0 Interceptions
(12/24, 50 Comp %)

2012 Notre Dame Fighting Irish 35

Tommy Rees #11
43 Yards, 1 Touchdown, 0 Interceptions
(4/4, 100 Comp %)

Rushing

Cierre Wood #20
66 Yards on 12 Carries
5.5 Yards per Carry
0 Touchdowns

Theo Riddick #6
45 Yards on 12 Carries
3.75 Yards per Carry
0 Touchdowns

Everett Golson #5
41 Yards on 15 Carries
2.73 Yards per Carry
0 Touchdowns

George Atkinson III #4
21 Yards on 3 Carries
7 Yards per Carry
0 Touchdowns

Receiving

Tyler Eifert #80
57 Yards on 4 Receptions
14.25 Yards per Reception
1 Touchdown

T.J. Jones #7
52 Yards on 4 Receptions
13 Yards per Reception
1 Touchdown Reception

Theo Riddick #6
38 Yards on 3 Carries
12.67 Yards per Carry
0 Touchdown Receptions

DeVaris Daniels #10
24 Yards on 2 Receptions
12 Yards per Reception
0 Touchdown Receptions

Kicking

Kyle Brindza #27
8 Points Total
2/2 Field Goals
2/2 Extra Points

Interceptions

Matthias Farley #41
1 Interception

Bennett Jackson #2
1 Interception

The Bottom Line

6 - 0

GAME 7

October 20, 2012
Notre Dame Stadium – Notre Dame, IN

Teams	1st	2nd	3rd	4th	Total
BYU	0	14	0	0	14
#5 Notre Dame	7	0	3	7	17

GAME SUMMARY

The seventh week of the 2012 season pitted 5th-ranked Notre Dame against an unranked and 4-3 Brigham Young University Cougars team.

The game started as most thought it would with Notre Dame taking a 7-0 lead. What was unexpected was BYU's unanswered 14 points in the 2nd quarter. The Fighting Irish defense held BYU to 0 zero points in the other 3 quarters. If it weren't for their offensive flurry in the 2nd quarter, BYU would have been shut out.

The Notre Dame rushing game was strong in this contest with both Theo Riddick and Cierre Wood rushing for over a hundred yards.

On the receiving front, Tyler Eifert was the most popular quarterback target as he racked up 73 yards and 1 touchdown on 4 receptions.

It's notable that Tommy Rees was the starting quarterback in place of Everett Golson, who was injured.

Notre Dame won the turnover war 2-1 (all were interceptions), but they lost the penalty battle, racking up 51 penalty yards to the Cougars' 35. Time of possession was close between both teams, but the Fighting Irish won total yards hands-down with 389 yards to BYU's 243 yards.

This game sparked some criticism that Notre Dame let even easy teams stay in the game for far too long, not putting them away fast enough. By the season's end, the Fighting Irish would prove those criticisms to be wrong.

Team Leaders

Passing

Tommy Rees #11
117 Yards, 1 Touchdown, 1 Interception
(7/16, 43.75 Comp %)

Andrew Hendrix #12
2 Yards, 0 Touchdowns, 0 Interceptions
(1/1, 100 Comp %)

Rushing

Theo Riddick #6
143 Yards on 15 Carries
9.53 Yards per Carry
0 Touchdowns

Cierre Wood #20
114 Yards on 18 Carries
6.33 Yards per Carry
0 Touchdowns

George Atkinson III #4
11 Yards on 5 Carries
2.2 Yards per Carry
1 Touchdown

Receiving

Tyler Eifert #80
73 Yards on 4 Receptions
18.25 Yards per Reception
1 Touchdown

T.J. Jones #7
40 Yards on 2 Receptions
20 Yards per Reception
0 Touchdowns

Kicking

Kyle Brindza #27
5 Points Total
1/3 Field Goals
2/2 Extra Points

Interceptions

Manti Te'o #5
1 Interception

Danny Spond #13
1 Interception

THE BOTTOM LINE

7 - 0

GAME 8

October 27, 2011
Oklahoma Memorial Stadium – Norman, OK

Teams	1st	2nd	3rd	4th	Total
#8 Oklahoma	3	3	0	7	7
#5 Notre Dame	7	3	0	20	38

GAME SUMMARY

This was a highly-touted matchup in which the 8th-ranked Oklahoma Sooners were facing off against the undefeated and 5th-ranked Notre Dame Fighting Irish. This was the game in which many know-it-all critics thought Notre Dame were finally going to fall apart under the pressure of a solid opponent. Boy, were they wrong.

This was a fairly close game, remaining 10-6 with Notre Dame holding a 4-point lead after a scoreless 3rd quarter. That was until Notre Dame ran away with the game in the 4th quarter, scoring 20 points and winning the game by a 17-point margin.

Total offensive yards were fairly close between the teams, with Notre Dame in the lead at 403 yards, and Oklahoma trailing close behind with 379 yards.

The total yard facts are a bit deceiving in this game in that it looks like both teams played a similar game and matched up nearly equally. Wrong. For starters Oklahoma was much more successful with their passing game, throwing for 364 yards to Notre Dame's 188 yards, nearly doubling their opponent's air attack. However, it was a much different story on the ground. Notre Dame's powerful defense held the Sooners to only 15 rushing yards, while their own offense racked up 215 running yards. By comparison, Oklahoma passed for 176 yards more yards, but the Fighting Irish ran for 200 yards more than their opponent. That gives Notre Dame a 24-yard advantage, leaving the teams nearly equal on offense, albeit with one excelling in the air and the other on the ground.

With nearly even yardage, how did the Irish win by 17 points? Notre Dame was nearly twice as effective on third down as was Oklahoma, which goes a long way to turning yardage on the field into points on the scoreboard. Notre Dame also had no turnovers. Nothing wastes offensive yards more than throwing the ball away.

While there were no passing touchdowns in this game, there was an exciting 50-yard pass to wide receiver Chris Brown.

Racking up 3 rushing touchdowns, it was another banner day for the Notre Dame running game. Riddick, Wood, and quarterback Everett Golson all rushed into the end zone against the Sooners.

Notre Dame won the turnover battle 1-0, and they only surrendered 5 yards on a lone penalty, while Oklahoma had 5 penalties for 39 yards.

TEAM LEADERS

Passing

Everett Golson #5
177 Yards, 0 Touchdowns, 0 Interceptions
(13/25, 52 Comp %)

Tommy Rees #11
11 Yards, 0 Touchdowns, 0 Interceptions
(1/1, 100 Comp %)

Rushing

Theo Riddick #6
74 Yards on 19 Carries
3.89 Yards per Carry
1 Touchdown

Cierre Wood #20
74 Yards on 7 Carries
10.57 Yards per Carry
1 Touchdown

Everett Golson #5
64 Yards on 11 Carries
5.82 Yards per Carry
1 Touchdown

Receiving

T.J. Jones #7
55 Yards on 5 Receptions
11 Yards per Reception
0 Touchdowns

Chris Brown #2
50 Yards on 1 Reception
50 Yards per Reception
0 Touchdowns

DaVaris Daniels #10
36 Yards on 2 Receptions
18 Yards per Reception
0 Touchdowns

Tyler Eifert #80
22 Yards on 3 Receptions
7.33 Yards per Reception
0 Touchdowns

Kicking

Kyle Brindza #27
12 Points Total
3/4 Field Goals
3/3 Extra Points

Interceptions

Manti Te'o #5
1 Interception

THE BOTTOM LINE

8 - 0

GAME 9

November 3, 2012
Notre Dame Stadium – Notre Dame, IN

Teams	1st	2nd	3rd	4th	OT	Total
Pittsburgh	3	7	10	0	6	26
#3 Notre Dame	3	3	0	14	9	29

GAME SUMMARY

The 9th game of the 2012 season was supposed to be an easy one for the 8-0 #1-ranked Notre Dame Fighting Irish as they faced a 4-4 unranked Pittsburgh team at home. Apparently, someone forgot to tell Pittsburgh it was supposed to be an easy game.

This game was a close contest from the beginning with Pittsburgh and Notre Dame both scoring field goals to tie in the first quarter and ending the second quarter with the Fighting Irish trailing the Panthers 6-10.

The third quarter was a bit of a shock as the Pittsburgh Panthers scored 10 unanswered points on the favorite Fighting Irish, extending their lead to 14 points. The fourth quarter, however, was all Notre Dame as they scored 2 unanswered touchdowns to tie the score and send the game into overtime.

Notre Dame won the total yards 522 to 308, passing yards 291 to 164, and rushing yards 231 to 144. Penalty yardage was nearly identical, Notre Dame with 46 yards on 6 penalties and Pittsburgh with 46 yards on 7 penalties.

So if Notre Dame won the yardage fight in the air and on the ground, what kept Pittsburgh in this game? They won the turnover battle. The Panthers did not turn over the ball once, and both Everett Golson and Tommy Rees threw an interception. On top of that, the Fighting Irish also lost a fumble. Usually when a team turns the ball over 3 times without taking the ball away from their opponent, the team loses the game. While the Fighting Irish didn't lose, these costly mistakes kept an inferior Pittsburgh team in the game far longer than they should have, all the way through 3 overtime periods.

While some critics faulted the Fighting Irish for allowing such a fight from an unranked team who already had 4 losses on their record and should easily have been put away by a #3 team, this game embodied the spirit of the 2012 Notre Dame Fighting Irish. Most teams who find themselves down 20-6 in the 4th quarter do not have the heart and fight to mount a comeback and tie up the game. The 2012 Fighting Irish never gave up and found a way to make the seemingly impossible work all year long, such as in the goal line stand against Stanford. This is the trademark of this team, and it's the reason why they went undefeated, despite all odds, and earned a shot at the 2013 BCS National Championship Game.

TEAM LEADERS

Passing

Everett Golson #5
227 Yards, 2 Touchdowns, 1 Interception
(23/42, 54.76 Comp %)

Tommy Rees #11
64 Yards, 0 Touchdowns, 1 Interception
(6/11, 54.55 Comp %)

Rushing

Theo Riddick #6
85 Yards on 22 Carries
3.86 Yards per Carry
0 Touchdowns

Everett Golson #5
74 Yards on 15 Carries
4.93 Yards per Carry
1 Touchdown

Cierre Wood #20
70 Yards on 13 Carries
5.38 Yards per Carry
0 Touchdowns

Receiving

DaVaris Daniels #10
86 Yards on 7 Receptions
12.29 Yards per Reception
0 Touchdowns

Tyler Eifert #80
62 Yards on 6 Receptions
10.33 Yards per Reception
0 Touchdowns

T.J. Jones #7
53 Yards on 5 Receptions
10.6 Yards per Reception
1 Touchdown

Robby Toma #9
50 Yards on 6 Receptions
8.33 Yards per Reception
0 Touchdowns

Theo Riddick #6
35 Yards on 4 Carries
8.75 Yards per Carry
1 Touchdown

Kicking

Kyle Brindza #27
9 Points Total
3/4 Field Goals
0/1 Extra Points

Interceptions

None

2012 Notre Dame Fighting Irish 53

THE BOTTOM LINE

THE BOTTOM LINE

9 - 0

GAME 10

November 10, 2012
Alumni Stadium – Chestnut Hill, MA

Teams	1st	2nd	3rd	4th	Total
Boston College	0	3	0	3	6
#4 Notre Dame	7	7	7	0	21

GAME SUMMARY

As a result of having trouble putting away unranked Pittsburgh Panthers in the previous week, Notre Dame was ranked down from #3 to #4, much to the ire of Fighting Irish fans.

With a 2-7 record coming into the game, the Boston College Eagles were not expected to be much competition for the Fighting Irish, and they weren't.

The scoring in this game can be described very easily. Notre Dame scored 1 touchdown in each of the 1st 3 quarters, while Boston College kicked 2 field goals – 1 in the 2nd quarter and 1 in the 4th. With a final score of 21-6, Notre Dame moved onto an 11-0 record, aimed squarely at making an appearance in the National Championship Game.

Boston College was a little more effective in the air than Notre Dame, passing for 247 yards to the Fighting Irish's 209 yards. The Fighting Irish once again won the ground battle, rushing for 184 yards while holding the Eagles to only 53 yards. This brings up the Fighting Irish total yardage to 393, topping Boston College's 300.

One of the keys to this victory was Notre Dame's amazing third down efficiency, being successful on 11 of 14 attempts, while the Eagles were effective on 8 of 15 third-down attempts. While Notre Dame did not try to convert any 4th downs, Boston College did and went 0 for 2 on those attempts.

While Notre Dame did not have a single interception, they did lose two fumbles to the Boston College Eagles. However, the Eagles did throw 1 interception and had 1 lost fumble, leaving the turnover war tied at 2-2.

Even if Boston College did not provide the toughest challenge for Notre Dame, this game was a good demonstration of the Fighting Irish's well-rounded abilities by chalking up 2 passing touchdowns from the hands of Everett Golson, along with his own rushing touchdown, converting 11 of 14 3rd-downs, stopping Boston College 2 of 2 times on 4th down, and grabbing yet another interception at the hands of Manti Te'o. That is a team firing on all cylinders, one that is capable of winning a national title.

TEAM LEADERS

Passing

Everett Golson #5
200 Yards, 2 Touchdowns, 0 Interceptions
(16/24, 62.5 Comp %)

Tommy Rees #11
9 Yards, 0 Touchdowns, 0 Interceptions
(1/1, 100 Comp %)

Rushing

Theo Riddick #6
104 Yards on 18 Carries
5.78 Yards per Carry
0 Touchdowns

Everett Golson #5
39 Yards on 11 Carries
3.54 Yards per Carry
1 Touchdown

Cierre Wood #20
33 Yards on 6 Carries
5.5 Yards per Carry
0 Touchdowns

Receiving

Tyler Eifert #80
67 Yards on 6 Receptions
11.17 Yards per Reception
0 Touchdowns

Theo Riddick #6
56 Yards on 4 Receptions
14 Yards per Reception
0 Touchdowns

T.J. Jones #7
39 Yards on 3 Receptions
13 Yards per Reception
0 Touchdowns

DaVaris Daniels #10
22 Yards on 2 Receptions
11 Yards per Reception
0 Touchdowns

John Goodman #81
18 Yards on 1 Reception
18 Yards per Reception
1 Touchdown Reception

Troy Niklas #85
7 Yards on 1 Reception
7 Yards per Reception
1 Touchdown Receptions

Kicking

Kyle Brindza #27
3 Points Total
0/0 Field Goals
3/3 Extra Points

Interceptions

Manti Te'o #5
1 Interception

THE BOTTOM LINE

10 - 0

DAN FATHOW 60

GAME 11

November 17, 2012
Notre Dame Stadium – Notre Dame, IN

Teams	1st	2nd	3rd	4th	Total
Wake Forest	0	0	0	0	0
#3 Notre Dame	21	10	7	0	38

GAME SUMMARY

In the previous week, the #1-ranked Alabama Crimson Tide were upset by the #15-ranked Texas A&M Aggies, causing them to drop down to #4 in the rankings and giving Notre Dame the opportunity to continue moving toward the nation's top spot. The Fighting Irish moved up to #3 and were facing an easy victory.

The Wake Forest Demon Deacons, unranked, came into the 11th game of the season with a 5-5 record and did not provide any challenge for the Fighting Irish who routed them 38-0. Considering that 31 of those points were scored before the half, this game was never really much of a contest. What it did provide for the Fighting Irish was an answer to critics who claimed that Notre Dame let inferior teams stay in the game too long, never really blowing anyone away. This game was not only a 38-point blowout, but a shutout, and it provided proof that Notre Dame can dominate a game as good as anyone.

This game was a slaughter from start to finish. Notre Dame won total yards 584 to 209, racking up much more than double the yardage of the Demon Deacons. The Fighting Irish rushed for 221 yards, 4 times the 55 yards put up by its opponent. The passing game wasn't much different with Notre Dame completing for 363 yards to Wake Forest's 154 yards.

TEAM LEADERS

Passing

Everett Golson #5
346 Yards, 3 Touchdowns, 1 Interception
(20/30, 66.67 Comp %)

Tommy Rees #11
17 Yards, 0 Touchdowns, 0 Interceptions
(2/5, 54.55 Comp %)

Rushing

Cierre Wood #20
150 Yards on 11 Carries
13.64 Yards per Carry
1 Touchdown

George Atkinson III #4
34 Yards on 7 Carries
4.86 Yards per Carry
1 Touchdown

Theo Riddick #6
20 Yards on 6 Carries
3.33 Yards per Carry
0 Touchdowns

Receiving

T.J. Jones #7
97 Yards on 6 Receptions
16.17 Yards per Reception
1 Touchdown

Tyler Eifert #80
85 Yards on 6 Receptions
14.17 Yards per Reception
1 Touchdown

John Goodman #81
59 Yards on 2 Receptions
29.5 Yards per Reception
1 Touchdown Reception

Theo Riddick #6
58 Yards on 3 Receptions
19.33 Yards per Reception
0 Touchdowns

Robby Toma #9
37 Yards on 2 Receptions
18.5 Yards per Reception
0 Touchdowns

Kicking

Kyle Brindza #27
8 Points Total
1/2 Field Goals
5/5 Extra Points

Interceptions

None

THE BOTTOM LINE

11 - 0

GAME 12

November 24, 2012
Los Angeles Coliseum – Los Angeles, CA

Teams	1st	2nd	3rd	4th	Total
USC	0	10	0	3	**13**
#1 Notre Dame	10	6	3	3	**22**

GAME SUMMARY

Finally. Finally. Finally, Notre Dame was the #1-ranked team in the entire country. Fighting Irish fans rejoiced that their team finally got the recognition it deserved. It took 11 hard fought victories to achieve that status, but they earned it.

The University of Southern California Trojans came into this game with a record of 7-4. They were certainly not expected to beat Notre Dame, but they were likely to be better competition than the Fighting Irish's previous two opponents. Even though Notre Dame never lost the lead, this was a closer game than the previous two contests.

Manti Te'o nabbed his 7th interception of the year, further spurring talk of his chances of winning the Heisman Trophy. Johnny Manziel, Texas A&M's star freshman quarterback, who was responsible for handing Alabama its only loss of the season, ended up winning the award with 2,029 points to Te'o's 1,706 points. It is notable that Te'o came closer to winning the coveted Heisman Trophy than any other strictly defensive player in history. Te'o did win 6 other national awards, which was a record in itself, not to mention he has a chance to win the national title. That is a pretty darn good senior year, even without the Heisman.

TEAM LEADERS

Passing

Everett Golson #5
217 Yards, 0 Touchdowns, 0 Interceptions
(15/26, 57.69 Comp %)

Rushing

Theo Riddick #6
146 Yards on 20 Carries
7.3 Yards per Carry
1 Touchdown

Everett Golson #5
47 Yards on 9 Carries
5.22 Yards per Carry
0 Touchdowns

Cierre Wood #20
20 Yards on 8 Carries
2.5 Yards per Carry
0 Touchdowns

Receiving

Tyler Eifert #80
69 Yards on 4 Receptions
17.25 Yards per Reception
0 Touchdowns

T.J. Jones #7
40 Yards on 3 Receptions
13.33 Yards per Reception
0 Touchdowns

Robby Toma #9
34 Yards on 2 Receptions
17 Yards per Reception
0 Touchdowns

Theo Riddick #6
33 Yards on 3 Receptions
11 Yards per Reception
0 Touchdowns

Kicking

Kyle Brindza #27
16 Points Total
5/6 Field Goals
1/1 Extra Points

Interceptions

Manti Te'o #5
1 Interception

KeiVarae Russell #6
1 Interception

THE BOTTOM LINE

12 - 0

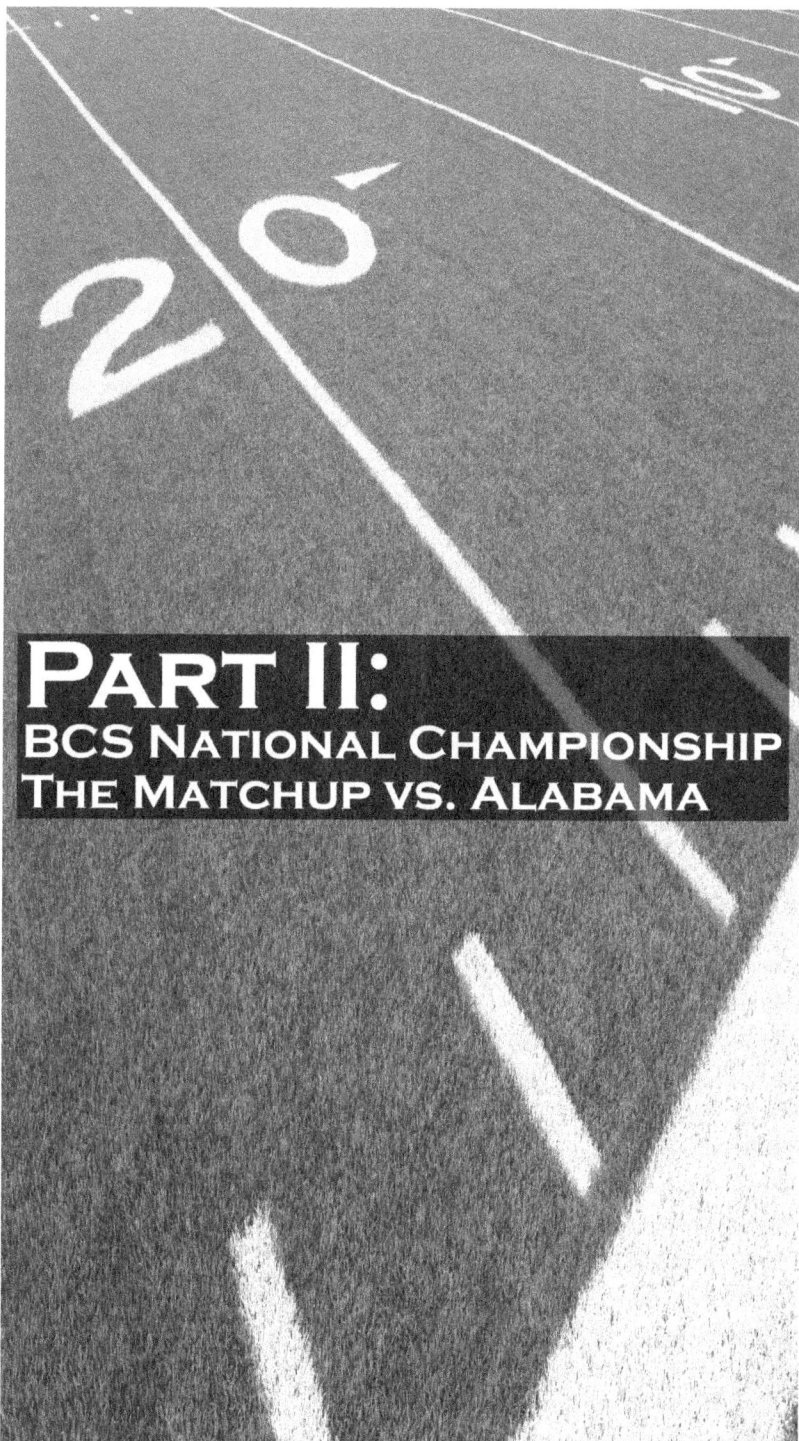

PART II:
BCS NATIONAL CHAMPIONSHIP
THE MATCHUP VS. ALABAMA

DAN FATHOW 70

Momentum, Advantages, & Minutiae

Wear & Tear

Alabama will have played 13 games going into the BCS Title Game on Monday, January 7, 2013, and they will have last played against Georgia in the SEC Championship on December 1st.

Notre Dame will have only played 12 games going into the BCS Title Game on January 7, 2013, and they will have last played against USC on November 24th.

What does this mean in relation to the BCS Championship Game?

Alabama will have played one more game than Alabama, having put their players through more wear and tear.

Advantage: Notre Dame

Time Off - Rust Factor vs Rest Factor

Notre Dame will have had 44 days off compared to Alabama's 37 Days off. So, Notre Dame has had one more week off than Alabama. More time off is not always a good thing. Whether the bye week in the NFL is beneficial or harmful has long been a debate among fans and commentators.

On advancednflstats.com, Denis O'Regan put together one of the best studies on this issue. After crunching a ton of numbers that are a bit irrelevant to this college football discussion, he came up with a conclusion that may be very relevant to the BCS Championship Game:

"Conclusion.

Favoured teams going on the road after a bye week appear to overperform by almost a field goal. This effect is largely absent in all other types of matchups."

(Denis O'Regan - Writer, Ed Anthony – Editor,
October 31, 2009
http://community.advancednflstats.com/2009/10/bye-weeks.html)

Okay, so that's an in-depth analysis of NFL teams' performances following a bye week. What does that have to do with the BCS Championship Game? Well, maybe nothing. Even if statistics are very strongly against something from happening in the sports world, there is a first time for everything, and there are no statistics that can prevent an athlete or a team to win in an underdog position. This very fact is probably what keeps us watching sports year after year. It's the chance that heart, determination, and hard work can make a champion out of someone that the world underestimated. And, by the same token, a tremendously talented team can lose to anyone if they grow overconfident, complacent, or take their opponent too lightly.

Okay, okay, so that's enough waxing poetic about the valor of sports. What does Mr. O'Regan's study mean for the BCS Championship Game?

Depending on where you look, Alabama is favored to win by between 8-10 points, even though Notre Dame is undefeated. The game is being held in Miami, FL, so both teams count as road teams in this scenario. If O'Regan's statistics hold true in the BCS title game, it would mean Alabama would score 3 more points than the expected spread predicts. If the experts are right, Alabama wins. In Notre Dame's defense, they have consistently been wrong about the Fighting Irish all year.

Advantage: *a slight maybe to Alabama*

TEAM PASSING STATISTICS

TEAM	Comp	Attempts	Comp %	Yards	TDs	Inter-ceptions
Alabama	199	300	66.3	2,788	27	3
Notre Dame	205	352	58.2	2,626	13	7

The obvious big difference in the passing department is that Alabama has double the touchdowns with less than half the interceptions. The advantage here obviously lies with the Crimson Tide.

TEAM RUSHING STATISTICS

TEAM	Carries	Yards	Average	Touchdowns
Alabama	525	2,920	5.6 Yards	35
Notre Dame	487	2,430	5 Yards	22

On one hand the rushing numbers are similar. Alabama has about 500 more yards, but they also took an extra 38 carries to get them. The yards per carry are close with Alabama earning 0.6 more yards per carry than Notre Dame. The big difference here is that Alabama picked up 13 more rushing touchdowns than the Fighting Irish during the regular season.

TEAM KICKING STATISTICS

TEAM	Extra Points	Extra Point %	Field Goals	Field Goal %	Total Points
Alabama	63	100	15	75	108
Notre Dame	31	94	24	75	103

The kicking game is probably the most balanced element between both teams. Alabama has a perfect extra point percentage, while Notre Dame has a 94% accuracy. On field goals, both teams have a 75% accuracy, but Notre Dame kicked 9 more field goals than Alabama. The total kicking points are nearly identical with Alabama at 108 and Notre Dame at 103. The kicking edge seems to lie a little more with Notre Dame being that Notre Dame kicked 60% more field goals than Alabama. Field goals will likely have more of an impact on a national title win than extra points.

TEAM DEFENSIVE TURNOVERS

TEAM	Interceptions	Fumbles
Alabama	17	4
Notre Dame	16	2

The defensive turnovers are nearly identical too, both teams having incredible defenses. Alabama has one more interception and two more fumbles, but it's too close to call to say either team has a true advantage here. Both teams have relied on their solid defenses and great turnover rates all year round, and they will surely play a vital role in deciding the winner of the 2013 BCS National Championship Game.

*Q*UARTERBACK *M*ATCHUP

McCARRON VS. GOLSON

By the numbers:

A.J. MCCARRON

Year	CMP	ATT	YDS	CMP%	TD	INT
2012	191	286	2669	66.8	26	3
2011	219	328	2634	66.8	16	5
2010	30	48	389	62.5	3	0

A.J. GOLSON

Year	CMP	ATT	YDS	CMP%	TD	INT
2012	166	282	2135	58.9	11	5

Even though Everett Golson has led Notre Dame through a fantastic season, AJ McCarron leads Golson in passing yards, completion percentage, touchdowns, and a far superior touchdown to interception ratio. While McCarron threw 8.67 touchdowns for every interception, Golson only threw 2.2 touchdowns for every interception. So McCarron threw nearly 4 times as many touchdowns per interception as his competitor during the regular season leading up to the BCS Title Game. Turnovers often decide football games; whether Golson can improve on these numbers or not in the big game could be the deciding factor.

EXPERIENCE

2012 was Everett Golson's first year as a starter, and during that year, he split a lot of games with Tommy Rees. A.J. McCarron has been the Crimson Tide's quarterback for 3 years, as the full-time starter the last 2 of those.

Besides the number of snaps and years of experience, there is also big game experience. Many players have found it difficult to perform in championship games in the same manner and at the same level as they had done all season. Press and media hoopla can unnerve many otherwise cool customers. Everett Golson, in his first year as a starter, has no previous experience in championship game pressure.

On the other hand, A.J. McCarron has already won a BCS Championship in 2012 against an undefeated LSU Tigers team, in New Orleans no less. In this game, McCarron led the Crimson Tide to a 21-0 victory while throwing for 234 yards on 23 completions on 34 attempts. In that game, McCarron did not throw a single interception.

If there is a criticism to be made of McCarron's performance in that victory, it is that he did not throw a single touchdown pass against a disoriented and poorly-performing LSU team. All of Alabama's points against LSU came in the form of 5 field goals by Jeremy Shelley and one rushing touchdown by

Trent Richardson. It is important to note that McCarron was without his top receiver, Marquis Maze, who left the field with a leg injury in the first quarter and was unable to return. Perhaps there would have been a McCarron to Maze touchdown pass if not for the injury. Regardless, not only has McCarron faced this pressure, but he has overcome it and excelled in spite of it.

So, Golson has not been to the big game before and neither does he have the experience of A.J. McCarron in the regular season. However, the entire 2012 season has been a series of challenges that Golson has risen to and met head on. Throughout the course of the season, Everett Golson has had to fight for his position as a starter against more experienced quarterback Tommy Rees. He's had to overcome an injury, and he's had to deal with the pressure of leading an underdog Notre Dame team through an undefeated season, including beating several ranked teams. It seemed every week the media and sports analysts were predicting Notre Dame's charmed winning streak would come to end, but it never did. Somehow, someway Golson led his team to victory, doing whatever it took in each specific situation for the Fighting Irish to get a mark in the win column. Overcoming higher-ranked teams and adversity has been no problem for Golson all season, so it's hard to count him out because he's facing a strong defense and a quarterback with more experience who has already won a national championship. It would seem the entire 2012 season was a preparation for Golson to meet this last challenge.

So, who's going to have the better day? Who is going to win the championship for their team?

Well, winning the championship is absolutely a team effort, so it's a bit cheeky to say either quarterback has that power alone. However, it's undeniable that a great quarterback performance, especially one with zero turnovers, can help lead a team to victory. If you're going by the numbers alone, it's likely that McCarron will put up better stats and help put the Crimson Tide on top. If you're going by Golson's ability to accomplish whatever needed to be done to win, it's likely that Golson may perform better in the clutch, maybe enough to put the Fighting Irish on top. Golson is not likely to beat McCarron on stats, but it is likely that he'll deliver on key plays. The danger with Golson is that if this game follows the regular season stats, he may throw more interceptions, which can easily give the game away to a capable team like Alabama.

What's most likely to happen is that two great quarterbacks and team leaders will both have a great day, providing an exciting and memorable championship game.

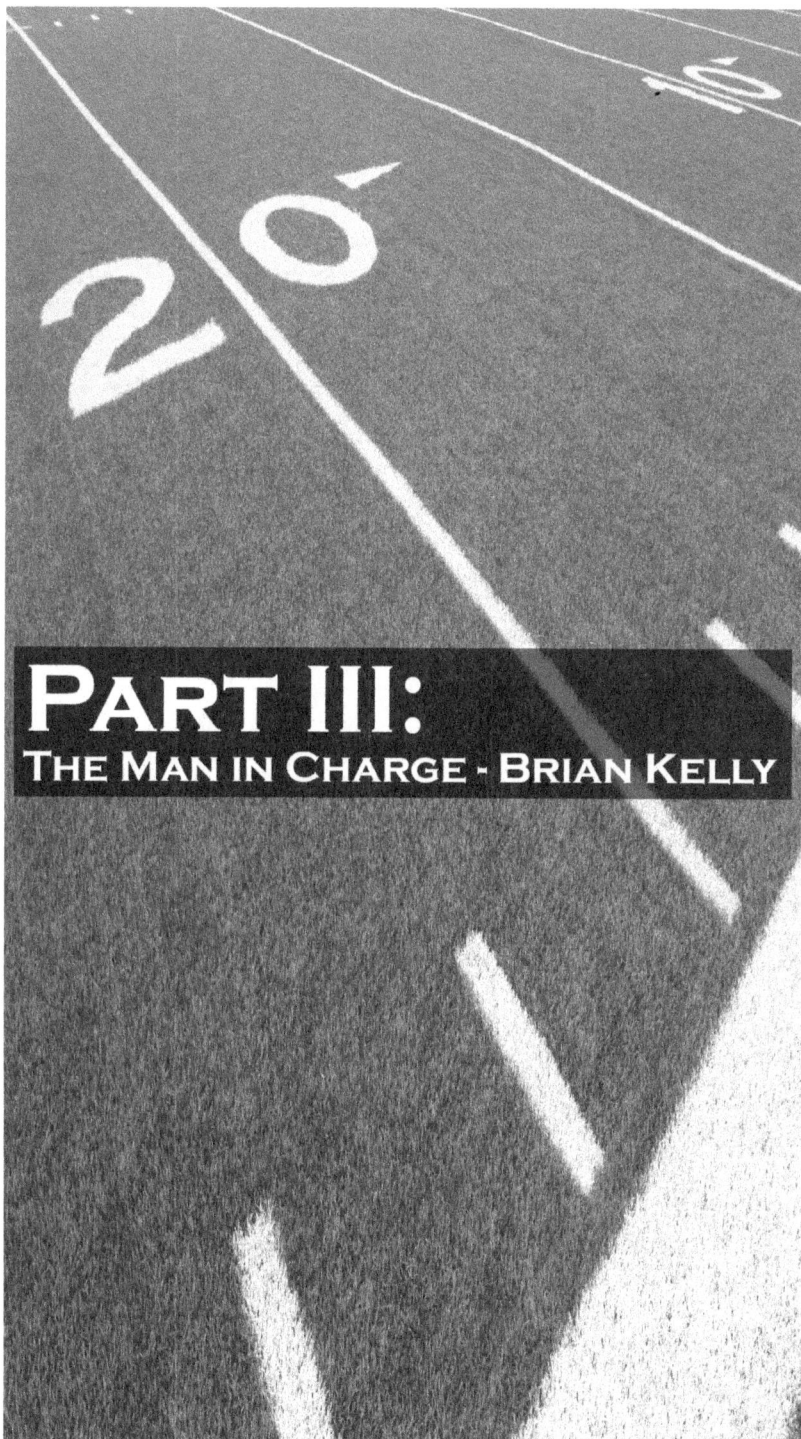

PART III:
THE MAN IN CHARGE - BRIAN KELLY

THE MAN IN CHARGE: HEAD COACH
BRIAN KELLY

If any casual college football fan didn't know who Brian Kelly was before the 2012 season, they certainly knew who he was by the time it was over, leading the unranked Notre Dame Fighting Irish through upset after upset, going undefeated, earning the #1-ranking in the nation, and securing a spot in the BCS Championship Game on January 7, 2013.

The truth is Brian Kelly was a highly successful, championship coach long before 2012.

Going back a ways...

In 1987, Brian Kelly became a defensive back coach for the Grand Valley State University Lakers. Quickly, Kelly moved up to defensive coordinator and recruiting coordinator in 1989. By 1991, Kelly became the team's head coach, beginning a long and successful coaching career.

For 13 years, Kelly coached the Lakers to great success, including national championships.

Year	Team	Overall	Standing	Bowl/playoffs
1991	Grand Valley State	9–3	T–2nd	*Loss NCAA Division II First Round*
1992	Grand Valley State	8–3	T–1st	
1993	Grand Valley State	6–3–2	3rd	
1994	Grand Valley State	8–4	2nd	*Loss NCAA Division II First Round*
1995	Grand Valley State	8–3	2nd	
1996	Grand Valley State	8–3	2nd	
1997	Grand Valley State	9–2	T–1st	
1998	Grand Valley State	9–3	1st	*Loss: NCAA Division II First Round*

1999	Grand Valley State	5–5	7th	
2000	Grand Valley State	7–4	3rd	
2001	Grand Valley State	13–1	1st	*Loss: NCAA Division II Championship*
2002	Grand Valley State	14–0	1st	**Win:** NCAA Division II Championship
2003	Grand Valley State	14–1	2nd	**Win:** NCAA Division II Championship
Grand Valley State:		118–35–2		

BRIAN KELLY COLLEGIATE HEAD COACHING RECORD – NCAA DIVISION I

Season	College	Record	Bowl Game
2004	Central Michigan	04-07	
2005	Central Michigan	06-05	
2006	Central Michigan	09-04	
2006	Cincinnati	01-00	**WIN – International Bowl**
2007	Cincinnati	10-03	**WIN – PapaJohns.com Bowl**
2008	Cincinnati	11-03	*LOSS – Orange Bowl*
2009	Cincinnati	12-00	
2010	Notre Dame	08-05	**WIN – Sun Bowl**
2011	Notre Dame	08-05	*LOSS – Champs Sports Bowl*
2012	Notre Dame	12-00	BCS (TBD)
ALL	**ALL**	**81-32**	03-02 in Bowl Games

BRIAN KELLY CENTRAL MICHIGAN HEAD COACHING RECORD

Seasons	College	Record	Win %	Bowl Game Record
2004-2006	Central Michigan	19-16	54.29 %	0-0

BRIAN KELLY CINCINNATI HEAD COACHING RECORD

Seasons	College	Record	Win %	Bowl Game Record
2006-2009	Cincinnati	34-06	85 %	2-1

BRIAN KELLY NOTRE DAME HEAD COACHING RECORD

Seasons	College	Record	Win %	Bowl Game Record
2010-2012	Notre Dame	28-10	73.68 %	1-1 (not including 2013 BCS)

Notre Dame Fighting Irish Players

by the Numbers

Number	Name	Position	Height	Weight	Year
1	Gunner Kiel	QB	6'4"	210	SO
2	Chris Brown	WR	6'2"	172	FR
2	Bennett Jackson	CB	6'1"	185	JR
3	Amir Carlisle	RB	5'10"	185	SO
4	George Atkinson III	RB	6'1"	210	SO
4	Eilar Hardy	S	5'11"	185	SO
5	Everett Golson	QB	6'1"	185	SO
5	Manti Te'o	LB	6'2"	255	SR
6	Theo Riddick	RB	5'11"	200	SR
6	KeiVarae Russell	CB	5'11"	182	FR
7	TJ Jones	WR	5'11"	190	JR
7	Stephon Tuitt	DE	6'6"	303	SO
8	Kendall Moore	LB	6'1"	242	JR

9	Louis Nix III	DL	6'3"	326	JR
9	Robby Toma	WR	5'9"	185	SR
10	DaVaris Daniels	WR	6'2"	190	SO
11	Tommy Rees	QB	6'2"	210	JR
11	Ishaq Williams	LB	6'5"	255	SO
12	Andrew Hendrix	QB	6'2"	220	JR
13	Danny Spond	LB	6'2"	248	JR
14	Luke Massa	WR	6'4"	225	JR
15	Dan McCarthy	S	6'2"	205	SR
16	Chris Badger	S	6'1"	193	FR
17	Charlie Fiessinger	QB	6'1"	185	SO
17	Zeke Motta	S	6'2"	215	SR
18	Ben Koyack	TE	6'5"	253	SO
19	Davonte' Neal	WR	5'9"	171	FR
20	Cierre Wood	RB	6'1"	215	SR

21	Jalen Brown	CB	6'1"	199	SO
22	Elijah Shumate	S	6'1"	198	FR
23	Lo Wood	CB	5'10"	195	JR
24	Chris Salvi	S	5'10"	190	SR
26	Jamoris Slaughter	S	6'1"	200	SR
27	Kyle Brindza	K	6'1"	225	SO
28	Austin Collinsworth	S	6'1"	202	JR
29	Nicky Baratti	S	6'1"	206	FR
30	Ben Councell	LB	6'5"	240	SO
31	John Turner	S	6'2"	207	FR
32	Will Mahone	RB	5'10"	211	FR
33	Cam McDaniel	CB	5'10"	195	SO
34	C.J. Prosise	S	6'2"	208	FR
35	Joe Romano	CB	5'9"	175	JR
35	Ben Turk	P	5'11"	186	SR
36	Will Salvi	CB	5'10"	176	SR

37	Eric Lee	WR	5'9"	180	SO
38	Nick Fitzpatrick	WR	5'8"	170	SR
38	Joe Schmidt	LB	6'1"	230	SO
39	Ryan Liebscher	WR	5'11"	205	JR
39	Jude Rhodes	P	5'10"	180	JR
40	Nick Tausch	K	6'1"	201	SR
41	Matthias Farley	S	5'11"	200	SO
42	Ernie Soto	S	5'9"	188	SO
43	Josh Atkinson	CB	5'11"	185	SO
44	Carlo Calabrese	LB	6'1"	245	SR
45	Romeo Okwara	LB	6'4"	239	FR
46	Josh Anderson	WR	5'9"	180	FR
46	Eamon McOsker	S	6'1"	200	FR
47	Connor Cavalaris	S	5'10"	194	SO
48	Dan Fox	LB	6'3"	240	SR

49	Blake Breslau	S	5'10"	185	SR
49	Tyler Plantz	RB	5'9"	202	JR
50	Chase Hounshell	DE	6'4"	275	SO
51	Bruce Heggie	C	6'5"	285	JR
52	Braxston Cave	C	6'3"	304	SR
53	Justin Utupo	DE	6'1"	258	JR
54	Kevin Walsh	LB	6'3"	220	SR
55	Prince Shembo	LB	6'2"	250	JR
56	Anthony Rabasa	LB	6'3"	240	SO
57	Mike Golic Jr.	C	6'3"	300	SR
59	Jarrett Grace	LB	6'3"	240	SO
60	Jordan Cowart	LS	6'2"	230	SR
61	Scott Daly	LS	6'2"	245	FR
62	Matt Tansey	OL	6'6"	270	SR
63	Grant Patton	DE	6'6"	256	SR
64	Tate Nichols	OT	6'8"	320	JR

65	Conor Hanratty	G	6'5"	305	SO
66	Chris Watt	G	6'3"	310	SR
67	Kevin Carr	DE	6'7"	325	JR
69	Tony Springmann	DL	6'6"	300	SO
70	Zack Martin	OT	6'4"	304	SR
71	Dennis Mahoney	OT	6'7"	294	SR
72	Nick Martin	OT	6'4"	290	SO
73	Dan Furlong	OL	6'7"	250	FR
74	Christian Lombard	G	6'5"	309	JR
75	Mark Harrell	OL	6'4"	287	FR
77	Matt Hegarty	C	6'5"	296	SO
78	Ronnie Stanley	OL	6'6"	304	FR
80	Tyler Eifert	TE	6'6"	251	SR
81	John Goodman	WR	6'3"	215	SR
82	Justin Ferguson	WR	6'2"	196	FR

82	Alex Welch	TE	6'4"	250	JR
83	Gerard Martinez	WR	6'1"	200	FR
84	Andre Smith	WR	6'2"	190	SO
85	Troy Niklas	TE	6'7"	260	SO
86	Arturo Martinez	DE	6'4"	250	JR
87	Daniel Smith	WR	6'4"	215	JR
88	Jake Golic	TE	6'4"	245	SR
89	Kapron Lewis-Moore	DE	6'4"	306	SR
91	Sheldon Day	DE	6'2"	286	FR
92	Tyler Stockton	DL	6'1"	285	SR
93	Connor Little	LB	6'3"	225	SO
94	Jarron Jones	DE	6'5"	299	FR
96	Kona Schwenke	DE	6'4"	290	JR

Alabama Crimson Tide Players

by the Numbers

Number	Name	Position	Height	Weight	Year
1	Dee Hart	RB	5'9"	190	FR
2	DeAndrew White	WR	6'1"	185	SO
3	Sunseri, Vinnie	DB	6'1"	215	SO
4	T.J. Yeldon	RB	6'2"	216	FR
5	Chris Black	WR	5'11"	178	FR
5	Jeremy Shelley	K	5'10"	165	SR
6	Ha'Sean Clinton-Dix	DB	6'1"	209	SO
6	Blake Sims	RB	6'1"	212	SO
7	Ryan Anderson	LB	6'2"	252	FR
7	Kenny Bell	WR	6'1"	180	JR
8	Cyrus Jones	WR	5'10"	192	FR
8	Jeoffrey Pagan	DL	6'4"	285	SO
9	Amari Cooper	WR	6'1"	198	FR
10	John Fulton	DB	6'1"	187	JR

2012 Notre Dame Fighting Irish 95

10	AJ McCarron	QB	6'4"	210	JR
11	Alec Morris	QB	6'3"	225	FR
11	Tana Patrick	LB	6'3"	236	JR
12	Phillip Ely	QB	6'1"	198	FR
13	Deion Belue	DB	5'11"	179	JR
13	Ty Reed	QB	6'1"	190	JR
14	Edward Aldag	QB	6'1"	183	FR
15	Eddie Williams	WR	6'3	204	FR
16	Bradley Sylve	DB	5'11	178	FR
17	Caleb Castille	DB	5'11	170	SO
17	Kenyan Drake	RB	6'1	204	FR
17	Parker Philpot	DB	5'10	180	JR
18	Levi Cook	DB	5'10	190	SR
18	Reggie Ragland	LB	6'2	247	FR
18	Nick Williams	WR	5'10	185	JR
19	Jonathan Atchison	LB	6'3	236	JR

19	Dustin Ellison	QB	6'1	180	SO
20	Nathan McAlister	WR	5'11	165	SR
20	Jarrick Williams	DB	6'1	212	JR
21	Brent Calloway	LB	6'1	217	FR
21	Bryson Moultry	DB	6'0	185	SO
21	Ranzell Watkins	DB	5'9	172	JR
22	Hunter Bush	DB	5'11	195	SR
22	Christion Jones	WR	5'11	185	SO
23	Taylor Morton	DB	5'11"	185	SO
23	Jabriel Washington	DB	5'11"	183	FR
24	Geno Smith	DB	6'1"	182	FR
25	Dillon Lee	LB	6'4"	240	FR
26	Landon Collins	DB	6'1"	202	FR
27	Nick Perry	DB	6'1"	208	JR
28	Dee Milliner	DB	6'1"	199	JR
29	Cody Mandell	P	6'4"	202	JR

30	Denzel Devall	LB	6'2"	243	FR
31	Jerrod Bierbower	DB	6'1"	185	SO
31	Kelly Johnson	TE	6'3"	230	SR
32	C.J. Mosley	LB	6'2"	232	JR
32	Trey Roberts	RB	6'1"	189	FR
33	Trey DePriest	LB	6'2"	245	SO
33	Marcus Polk	WR	5'8"	180	SO
34	Ben Howell	RB	5'9"	194	SR
34	Tyler Owens	LB	6'1"	220	SO
35	Nico Johnson	LB	6'3"	245	SR
36	Tyler Hayes	LB	6'2"	210	FR
37	Robert Lester	DB	6'2	210	SR
40	Spencer Duncan	RB	6'2	230	SO
41	Kurt Freitag	TE	6'4	240	FR
42	Adrian Hubbard	LB	6'6	248	SO
42	Eddie Lacy	RB	6'1	220	JR

43	Cade Foster	K	6'1	218	JR
44	LaMichael Fanning	DL	6'7	298	FR
45	Jalston Fowler	RB	6'1	242	JR
46	Michael Nysewander	TE	6'1	230	SO
46	Wilson Whorton	P	5'10	175	SO
47	Xzavier Dickson	LB	6'3	262	SO
47	Corey McCarron	TE	6'2	240	SO
48	Rowdy Harrell	LB	6'1	221	SR
49	Ed Stinson	DL	6'4	282	JR
50	Alphonse Taylor	DL	6'5	340	FR
51	Wilson Love	DL	6'3	281	FR
51	Carson Tinker	LS	6'1	220	SR
52	MK Taylor	LS	5'10	210	JR
52	Dalvin Tomlinson	DL	6'2	266	FR
53	Anthony Orr	DL	6'4"	258	SO
54	Russell Raines	OL	6'2"	277	JR

54	Jesse Williams	DL	6'4"	320	SR
55	Josh Dickerson	LB	6'1"	238	SO
56	William Ming	DL	6'3"	283	JR
57	Aaron Joiner	OL	6'2"	265	SR
57	D.J. Pettway	DL	6'2"	285	FR
58	Brandon Greene	OL	6'5"	292	FR
59	Harold Nicholson	OL	6'5"	292	SO
61	Anthony Steen	OL	6'3"	303	JR
62	Brandon Ivory	DL	6'4"	315	SO
63	Kellen Williams	OL	6'3"	303	JR
64	Michael Newsome	DL	6'2"	250	SO
65	Chance Warmack	OL	6'3"	320	SR
67	Alex Shine	OL	6'3"	300	FR
68	Isaac Luatua	OL	6'2"	313	FR
69	Paul Waldrop	OL	6'4"	267	FR
70	Ryan Kelly	OL	6'5	288	FR

71	Cyrus Kouandjio	OL	6'6	311	SO
74	Caleb Gulledge	OL	6'4	280	FR
75	Barrett Jones	OL	6'5	302	SR
76	D.J. Fluker	OL	6'6	335	JR
77	Arie Kouandjio	OL	6'5	310	SO
78	Chad Lindsay	OL	6'2	290	SO
79	Austin Shepherd	OL	6'5	312	SO
80	Marvin Shinn	WR	6'3	198	FR
81	Danny Woodson	WR	6'1	195	FR
82	Harrison Jones	TE	6'4	244	SO
83	Kevin Norwood	WR	6'2	195	JR
84	Brian Vogler	TE	6'7	258	SO
85	Malcolm Faciane	TE	6'5	259	FR
85	Korren Kirven	DL	6'5	292	FR
87	Parker Barrineau	WR	6'1	175	SO

2012 Notre Dame Fighting Irish 101

88	Josh Magee	WR	6'1	170	FR
89	Michael Williams	TE	6'6	269	SR
90	Quinton Dial	DL	6'6"	304	SR
92	Damion Square	DL	6'3"	286	SR
93	Chris Bonds	DL	6'4"	273	JR
94	Dakota Ball	DL	6'2"	295	FR
95	Darren Lake	DL	6'3"	315	FR
98	Dillon Drake	K	5'9"	175	SO
99	Adam Griffith	K	5'10"	174	FR

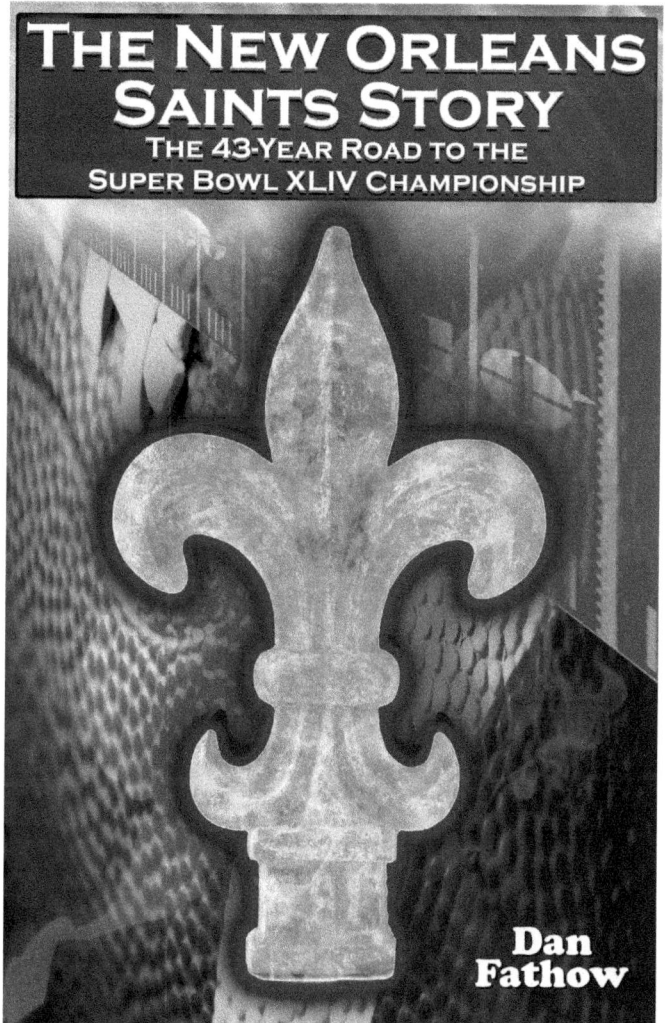

ALSO BY DAN FATHOW
STEINBRENNER: QUOTES, HITS, & LEGACY

Ever want to know what past-enemies Billy Martin, Yogi Berra, and Dave Winfield thought of their feuds with Steinbrenner? Want to know what Don Mattingly had to say following Steinbrenner's passing? Topics discussed range from Big Stein's suspension and subsequent lifetime ban from baseball; to his famous *Seinfeld* appearances, to Steinbrenner candidly commenting on his own flaws; to the appreciation of those he's helped over the years; to Steinbrenner's views on business, life philosophy, and charity; to criticisms of those he's scorned, to the numerous comments on his legacy from managers (Joe Torre, Lou Piniella, Joe Girardi), politicians (Bill Clinton, Rudy Giuliani), and current and former players (Derek Jeter, Wade Boggs, Darryl Strawberry, & many more). For an unbiased take on his life, Steinbrenner's stats as an owner are also crunched to give a factual perspective of his reign.

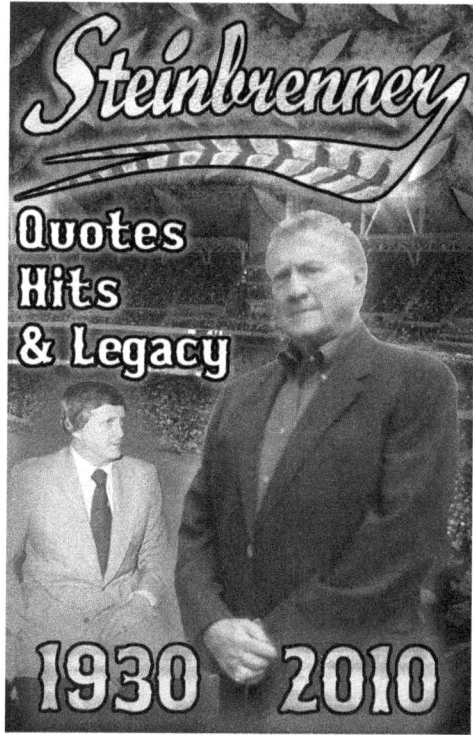

Steinbrenner's quotes cover such wide and interesting topics as Watergate, Pete Rose, Locker-Room Double Standards, Reggie Jackson, Alex Rodriguez, Yankee Tradition, Buying Championships, The Pine Tar Incident, General George S. Patton, His Alleged Fist-Fight with 2 Dodger Fans, and On How He'd Like to Be Remembered.

ISBN 978-0-9800605-7-7

www.ingramcontent.com/pod-product-compliance
Lightning Source LLC
Chambersburg PA
CBHW072205090426
42740CB00012B/2400